GOD'S PLAN FOR SHARING

North America: Your Mission Field

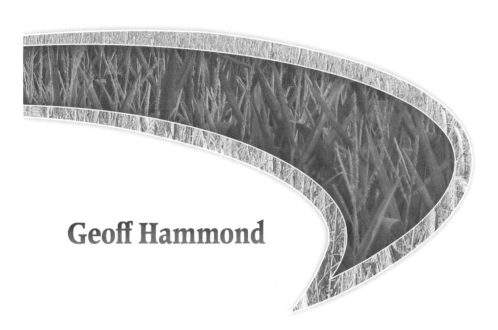

Geoff Hammond

Dedicated to my missionary parents Rothney and Brenda Hammond who gave most of their lives to sowing down the gospel in Africa.

"Jesus himself drew near, and went with them."
LUKE 24:15(B) KJV

This is the life verse given to my parents on their wedding day. It is a great reminder that as they sowed in the mission field, Jesus was right there with them.

Acknowledgements

No project is ever undertaken alone or completed without the assistance and collaboration of many friends and coworkers. I have been blessed with dedicated team members on this journey without whom this book could not have been completed. I could not have accomplished this without the encouragement and support of the entire North American Mission Board team.

I am very grateful to Bobby Sena for serving as project facilitator for the book, God's Plan for Sharing, and working in conjunction with the following team; Steve Reid, Brandon Pickett, Ken Weathersby, and Van Kicklighter in their continuous counsel in clarifying the communication of biblical principles and concepts in this book.

A special thanks to Tom Cheyney, Jerry Pipes, Dick Church, Van Sanders, Chris McNairy, Joshua Del Risco, Elaine Helms, and Mark Snowden for being major contributors to the development and writing of this book.

Thank you to Jill Owen and Clark Berryman for keeping us on task, and to Shawn Elledge for the cover design of the book.

Also, I would like to thank the following that served as readers and editors of the manuscript: Les Dobbins, Margaret Dempsey-Colson, Lisa Cheater, Sherri Jachelski, and Gaylynn Nieminen.

Above all, I want to thank our Lord and Savior Jesus Christ, and the thousands of Southern Baptist lay leaders, pastors, missionaries, prayer warriors, churches, director of missions, and state convention leaders that faithfully serve the Lord, share His gospel and invest their time, energy, and financial resources harvesting our North American mission field.

Dr. Geoff Hammond
President
North American Mission Board

{ EVERY BELIEVER SHARING }
{ EVERY PERSON HEARING }

Foreword

God is at work in North America. He is at work in the hearts of those who know Him and those who have yet to meet Him through a personal relationship with Jesus. I believe a paradigm shift in evangelism and missions is underway as our communities become more diverse with people groups representing a variety of worldviews. People with similar values, languages and worldviews are clustering in our major cities, and the way churches, believers, and missionaries go about the task of evangelism must change.

This book grows out of a passion to sow down North America with the gospel of the Lord Jesus to all people. Author Geoff Hammond has a special calling as a missionary, minister, missiologist, and president of the North America Mission Board. Through his experience, Geoff has a bird's-eye view of "lostness" in North America and brings to this subject a first-hand understanding of our changing, global society.

Born in Ogbomosho, Nigeria, to missionary parents, Geoff is a graduate of Spurgeon's Seminary in London, and received the Doctor of Ministry Degree in Evangelism and Missions from Southwestern Baptist Theological Seminary. He has served as a church planting strategist on two continents, and has held missions positions in Baptist churches and associations across the south, southeast and Texas. Geoff was senior associate director of the Southern Baptist Conservatives of Virginia until spring 2007, when he was elected by the Board of Trustees as president of the North American Mission Board.

Geoff's experience has prepared him for such a time as this: to unify and mobilize Southern Baptist churches in evangelizing the lost. Reading this book will invigorate your missions philosophy and theology. It will give you an honest appraisal of lostness in North America and the

{ EVERY BELIEVER SHARING }
{ EVERY PERSON HEARING }

Great Commission refocus that is needed in each community across our continent. To reach every person with the gospel, Geoff outlines a process called "GPS, God's Plan for Sharing." The vision of God's Plan for Sharing is every believer sharing, every person hearing the gospel in North America by the year 2020.

I hope and pray that, through these pages, you will allow God to challenge you and your church to be on mission with Him. In Acts 1:8, our Lord commissioned His followers to be witnesses in Jerusalem, in all of Judea and Samaria, and to the ends of the earth. We're asking you to join us in the North American mission field, and make salvation through Christ Jesus available to every person.

Ken Weathersby
Senior Strategist, Evangelization
North American Mission Board

Introduction

He's the guy in the business suit sitting next to you on the plane. She's the mother cheering beside you at the soccer game. They're the Hindu couple who just moved in two doors down. You connect with a smile, a few words of greeting. You may not know their names—but God does. He also cares deeply about their spiritual condition.

Do you?

Witnessing should come easy for me. After all, I grew up as a missionary kid. My life from birth to now has been missions-focused. I have the privilege of serving today as the president of Southern Baptists' North American Mission Board. In that role, I have the joy of joining with our staff, missionaries, and partners to reach North America for Christ—dispelling the deep spiritual darkness in the United States, Canada, and their territories.

Sharing the good news of Jesus Christ is my job, but it is also my joy—my passion. Yet, I know that I miss opportunities to do so. God continually prompts me to be bolder and more passionate in sharing my faith with others.

It's not always an easy task. In fact, in our culture today, it is uniquely challenging. But the call to fulfill the Great Commission is not merely an option for Christians. It is a requirement. Obedience to that call has eternal significance! Knowing that compels me to do everything possible, by every means possible, to share the good news of Jesus Christ with everyone, everywhere—starting at my own doorstep. A recent survey found that more than half of the respondents were willing to hear about Jesus if the discussion was with a family member, friend, or neighbor from the church.[1]

North America is unmistakably a mission field. Read a newspaper, listen to the radio, or surf the Internet and you'll quickly discover headlines

{ EVERY BELIEVER SHARING }
{ EVERY PERSON HEARING }

and stories that shout out all is not well. Sin is prevalent. Satan has a stronghold on so many lives. People are lost and without hope, wandering through spiritual darkness and needing someone to shed the light of Christ in their lives. No matter who they are, what they've done, or where they come from, these people need to know that the hope of Jesus Christ can be theirs. We as Christians are the only ones who can help them discover that hope.

People from nearly every nation are now our neighbors, and we are facing the challenge of a rapidly increasing population. With more than 300 million people in the United States, the projection is that the nation's population will grow to 440 million by 2050. Canada's population is now more than 30 million, and more than 250,000 immigrants are admitted each year.[2, 3]

If we are truly going to reach this continent, this mission field, with the gospel, we are going to have to work together more than ever before, talk to more people than ever before, and do things differently than we've ever done before. We do this not just because it's new and innovative, but also because North America's population is vastly different than what it was even ten years ago. Our society is more secular and pluralistic than ever.

While the population numbers seem daunting, for each number, there is a face and a name—a person whom God loves and who needs to know Jesus Christ as Lord and Savior. And, it is up to us to reach them so that the population of the kingdom of God will also grow! That's why I am excited about Southern Baptists' evangelism emphasis. God's Plan for Sharing (GPS) is that every believer is sharing and every person is hearing the gospel. It is living out the Great Commission in an intentional and passionate way. Imagine with me every person in North America hearing the gospel by 2020! Lives, families, communities, and churches will be changed—radically transformed by God's amazing power!

You received that power of Christ when you accepted Him as your Savior and Lord. I pray that you will join with me and countless others as we share that transforming power. We must do so with a sense of urgency. Consider this: one person dies every 11 seconds in North America, and three out of four people die without a personal relationship with Jesus Christ. That statistic grieves my heart, and I know it grieves the heart of God.[4]

God's Plan for Sharing is a timely evangelism emphasis to help us reach our neighbors and the nations for Jesus' sake. As you read this book, you will learn more about God's Plan for Sharing, and specifically the four key elements of this emphasis: Praying (*every* church praying for lost people), Engaging (*every* believer sharing as a trained witness), Sowing (*every* lost person receiving a witness), and Harvesting (*every* church harvesting and celebrating every salvation response). Note the emphasis on *every*. Not a one left out or left behind! It's a bold, God-sized goal, but should we settle for anything less?

The sheer size of the lost population in North America makes it the fourth largest mission field in the world.[5] To understand the magnitude of the challenge before us, imagine a farmer whom God has blessed with enough land to plant 100 rows of corn, but year after year he plants only 60 rows. Then the Lord gives the farmer more land. This extra amount of land will support planting another 100 rows of corn—200 rows total—but for some reason, the farmer continues to plant corn in only the original 60 rows.

Several more years pass, and God gives the farmer another 100 acres. The farmer is blessed with abundant harvests from the 60 rows that he does plant, so what keeps him from realizing that all the additional land will give him a much larger harvest? Inexplicably, the farmer continues to plant corn in only 60 rows of his field. He could plant in 300 rows, but he settles for that with which he is familiar and comfortable tending.

When the farmer eventually dies and goes to heaven, the Lord asks him, *Why did you only plant 60 rows every year? Didn't you see the 300 rows that I gave you?* The farmer has no answer for his behavior. He knows the

{ EVERY BELIEVER SHARING }
{ EVERY PERSON HEARING }

land was wasted, and he hangs his head in shame.

Many Christians in North America are just like that farmer.

No longer can we ignore the growing mission field all around us. Doing what we've always done will not create a new result. We are familiar with what's worked in the past, but now it's time to urgently sow down the gospel among all the peoples of North America.

As I travel around this continent, one of my great joys is to hear the incredible stories of how God is moving and working through Southern Baptists. It seems every time I have the privilege to preach or visit with a pastor, state or associational leader, or lay leader, I hear another testimony to God's amazing power. Throughout this book, you'll read some of these stories as well as some that I've collected from the staff of the North American Mission Board.

God has given you and me the land. He has provided the resources. Let us take to the field!

Dr. Geoff Hammond
President
North American Mission Board

CHAPTER ONE:
Lost in North America

Jesus is not anonymous. Many people in North America have heard of Him; many have not. They may know of Jesus and the era in which He lived. They may have even heard that Jesus loves them, but still they ask, *So? Who is He? Why does it matter?* As believers, it's difficult to fully grasp the idea that lost people living in North America may be familiar with the Savior, but they don't have any idea who Jesus really is and what His love means to their lives.

In the United States and Canada, lost people are made aware of the name "Jesus Christ" through a variety of media. Thousands of local churches, literally tons of literature, radio broadcasts and programs, the Internet, television, movies, Christian bookstores, seminaries, para-church ministries, and individual Christians, all use the name of Jesus. They represent hundreds, if not thousands, of theologically diverse affiliations and denominations. But to the lost, Jesus is just one more religious fanatic. They don't see Him as the answer to life's questions. "Lostness" is the lack of a *relationship* with Christ, not a lack of name recognition.

The Bible clearly directs us to purposefully let our life serve as a witness for Christ wherever we live and wherever we go:

> *You will receive power when the Holy Spirit has come upon you;*
> *and you shall be My witnesses both in Jerusalem,*
> *and in all Judea and Samaria, and even to the remotest*
> *part of the earth.*
> **ACTS 1:8**

{ EVERY BELIEVER SHARING }
{ EVERY PERSON HEARING }

Never before have people so desperately needed to hear the gospel in Canada and the United States than right now. The need is undeniable as we look around our culture.

Southern Baptists, indeed all Christians, must seize the kingdom opportunity before us and, with urgency, boldly share the good news of Jesus Christ with all the lost people living in our communities. The time is ripe for the harvest. It is time for the message of Christ to spread.

The early Christians were few in number, but they quickly made the name of Jesus recognized throughout the Mediterranean as they loved and worshipped Him as their Savior. Stunned, non-believers saw these early Christians as *"men who have upset the world."*[6]

May the same be said of us today in North America! We can turn our world upside down through the power of the gospel of Jesus Christ. We simply need to take the gospel to the spiritually lost all around us—men, women, boys, and girls—and invite them into a saving relationship with Christ.

Jesus Saw the Lost

In first-century Palestine, people began to hear about a man named Jesus. They heard about His love and miracles, but they were unsure about His objective: *Is He just a prophet, a political revolutionary, a carpenter, lunatic, or the Savior of the world?* When they were fortunate enough to meet Christ in person, many concluded that He was the answer to their yearnings for God. They understood. He had come for them.

The lost were Jesus' priority, every day. They were His reason for being. Referring to Himself, Jesus declared:

> *...the Son of Man has come to seek*
> *and to save that which was lost.*
> **Luke 19:10**

 GOD'S PLAN FOR SHARING | North America: Your Mission Field

Jesus used parables on several occasions to illustrate the concept of being lost. He talked about a sheep, a coin, and a son who all lost their way from the one who loved them. All three parables teach us that when something is lost, the owner must actively look for it or else it will remain lost forever.

The truth of these parables still holds true today in North America. The lost are only won to Christ when someone searches for them. Lost people do not know they are lost! They do not realize that Christ is searching for them by way of His witnesses. These parables also shine a bright light on the Savior's heart for all people. Jesus spoke of God's love to all kinds of people. He was willing to go to those most ignored and shunned by the majority—Hebrew culture of Israel. We, who love Christ and have His love within us, must demonstrate that same type of compassion for the lost, wherever, whenever, they cross our path.

Putting a Face on Lostness

Biblically, a lost person is one who does not have a personal relationship with God through Jesus Christ as Savior and Lord. The lost are blind to the truth of the gospel and are, therefore, unable to be in a relationship with their Creator. It is as though their ability to understand is covered with an impenetrable shell, and the truth and light of the gospel are hidden from them.

When I think about the specific people in my life who are without Christ, "lostness" ceases to be a spiritual concept; it becomes a death sentence. Spend a moment to personalize this reality with the faces of your lost friends or family members. As you picture their faces, envision their minds closed off from recognizing the light of the gospel in you. The Bible tells us that the gospel is light that shines brightly to illuminate the glory of God through the Christian believer.[7] Yet, your lost friend and mine cannot see nor understand it. Imagine the lost people in your social networks who

{ EVERY BELIEVER SHARING }
{ EVERY PERSON HEARING }

live each day in total spiritual darkness even though you are nearby, living in the light of the gospel. Does your heart yearn for them to know the truth and be set free from their darkness? Many share their situation.

Using our farming analogy from the introduction, each cornrow represents about a million people. The United States is the third most populated country in the world and Canada ranks 32nd. Among these countries, it is estimated that nearly 255 million people do not have a saving faith in Christ.[8] This means 255 rows need sowing! Yes, you heard correctly. About 229 million people in the United States and 26 million people in Canada have not accepted the gospel. And yet, like the farmer, most Southern Baptist churches continue to sow the gospel in the same familiar rows where a harvest has been plentiful over the past 50 years.

Why? We're not seeing North America as a mission field.

Developing Missionary Eyes

Like Jesus, we need to train our eyes to study lost people and their culture. The initial objective of a missionary when entering a new place is to observe the main characteristics of that culture. When we have missionary eyes for the United States and Canada, we notice things about our society we've never seen before, characteristics that impact our effectiveness in witnessing to the lost.

Change is all around us. Look closely at the community where you live, and you'll notice that change is a constant reality. Increasingly diverse populations, new varieties of spirituality and religion, urbanization, and rapid technological advancement are among the most prominent catalysts of change in North American life today. However, the nature of lostness is the same today as it was in the first century. Being lost still means spiritual darkness, without hope, joy, or peace, and living in the fear of death. Change is unavoidable, but it's also influential in creating new opportunities for the lost to hear the gospel.

Let's choose to view these changes as God-given opportunities for sowing the gospel in freshly cultivated soil. Change is good when it motivates the lost to consider their need for God and seek Him. The question for churches and believers is obvious. Will we see these cultural shifts as barriers to the gospel, or will we see the changing landscape as an opportunity to bring hope to those living in spiritual darkness?

Diverse Peoples and Religions

The United States and Canada are two of the most diverse countries in the world, and the emerging face of lostness in North America is tied closely to the diverse religious beliefs held by the people who immigrate here. The spiritual climate of each community changes as immigrants and their religious beliefs take root and spread throughout their new hometown. Christianity becomes just one of many religious options for the spiritual seeker.

Having been born, raised, and schooled outside the United States, I remember that it was both terrifying and exciting to relocate to a new city within a new country and culture. We were a missionary family, and we found comfort in our faith in Christ, but individuals moving here from another country that embraces a non-Christian religion don't have that security. They often settle together in groups, clinging to the culture and traditions that are familiar and comforting.

In his book, *Discipling Our Nation*, author Murray Moerman provided a picture of lostness in Canada by outlining five distinct mission fields there:

- **Established Postmoderns:** Mainstream Canadians who hold to relativism, pluralism, and the denial of any absolute truth.
- **New Canadians:** New immigrants who are mostly Muslim, Sikh, Buddhist, Hindu, and adherents to other religions.
- **French:** This group includes 6.5 million people and is the largest unreached people group in North America; fewer than one percent are Christian.

{ EVERY BELIEVER SHARING }
{ EVERY PERSON HEARING }

- **First Nations People:** The Canadian Indians.
- **Multi-family Housing:** Many of the previously mentioned groups live in this type housing that is often overlooked by the church for outreach.[9]

This list doesn't apply only to residents of Canada. Similar groups of lost people with diverse beliefs live in the United States as well. According to the 2007 Census, slightly more than 38 million foreign-born individuals were living in the United States, about 12.6 percent of the total U.S. population, with Mexican immigrants comprising almost one-third of that group. People from Latin America and Asia make up the majority of the remainder.[10]

Increasing numbers of immigrants from non-European countries are projected to significantly alter the ethnic ratios of the United States. Demographics expert and research professor at the University of Michigan, William Frey, recently noted:

> *The Census Bureau's new projections through 2050 portend a more accelerated transformation of the nation's population on race-ethnic dimensions than was previously supposed. These new projections show that the year when the white population dips to below half of the total will occur in 2042, 8 years sooner than in the Bureau's projections just 4 years ago. By 2050 the nation will be 46 percent white, down from 66 percent today, and 30 percent Hispanic, double the 15 percent we have today.*[11]

The influx of new people and non-Christian belief systems create a profound religious shift that impacts us all. In 2001, Diana Eck penned a book titled *A New Religious America: How a Christian Country Has Become the World's Most Religiously Diverse Nation.*

Eck paints a powerful portrait of the diverse religious landscape as follows:

> Envisioning the new America in the twenty-first century requires an imaginative leap. It means seeing the religious landscape of America, from sea to shining sea, in all its beautiful complexity. Between the white New England churches and the Crystal Cathedral of southern California, we see the sacred mountains and the homelands of the Native peoples, the Peace Pagoda amid maples in Massachusetts, the mosque in the cornfields outside Toledo, the Hindu temples pitched atop the hills of Pittsburgh and Chicago, the old and new Buddhist temples of Minneapolis. Most of us have seen too little of this new religious America.[12]

Can you see how the light of Christ can be diffused across our continent? It's our direct responsibility to point everyone to the one true Light. The people of all cultures are to be reached because Christ loves them and gave his life on a cross for them. They need to meet the Savior!

Churches have unprecedented opportunities to reach some of the least-evangelized peoples of the world without ever leaving the community. Will we look upon immigrants as foreigners, or will we see them with missionary eyes, just as Christ views and loves them?

Urbanization

The density and diversity of North American populations are most evident in urban settings. Approximately 200 million people live in 100 of the largest metropolitan areas in the United States. This represents 65 percent of the country's total population.[13] In Canada, 45 percent of the population lives in only eight metropolitan areas, where the influence of Christianity is declining.[14,15]

{ EVERY BELIEVER SHARING }
{ EVERY PERSON HEARING }

Urban contexts provide many challenges to planting the gospel and encouraging discipleship. Concentrated areas of poverty or wealth, multi-housing complexes, crime, gangs, and education patterns can impede effective sowing of the gospel in urban areas. It's hard to find a traditional church in population-dense areas. There simply isn't space or interest. This means that the closest churches may be smaller, more relational, or meet in community buildings.

Urbanization is also impacting the suburbs. Bruce Katz, founding director for the Metropolitan Policy Program, believes that suburbs as we know them are vanishing.[16] He argued that suburbs no longer represent a retreat from the tumult of American life, but are fast becoming the focus of it:

> *Suburbs now provide more jobs than cities. Only about 22 percent of jobs in major metropolitan areas are located within three miles of a traditional downtown; twice as many are more than 10 miles out. Suburbs also host more immigrants: in the largest metropolitan areas, nearly six in 10 foreign-born residents now live in the suburbs. In places like Charlotte, N.C., Minneapolis, Sacramento, Calif., and Washington, the first address of many new Americans is most likely down a suburban lane. Nationwide, a million more suburbanites are living below the poverty line than city dwellers. What do we do now that they resemble our cities, in good ways and bad?*[17]

Technology

Technological advances have turned the once unimaginable idea of a "glocal community" into a reality. Used in this context, the term "glocal" refers to a community that is willing and able to think globally, but act locally. The ability to connect with people throughout the world via the Internet dramatically shrinks the communication distance around the globe. There are certainly benefits of being able to relay information around the world in real-time; however, technology also can take the place of personal, face-to-face relationships.

Technology seems to evolve faster than we can purchase it. We've moved so far beyond simple email. More and more people are experiencing virtual communities on the Internet. They use chat-room forums, Vblogging, Skype, Facebook, MySpace, Twitter and other venues to maintain and develop relationships. Individual Christians and churches need to take their witness into these formats to reach the lost person who prefers to communicate online. Evangelistic methodologies must include these growing electronic social networks if we are to impact lostness in every way possible.

While the evangelism challenge before us is sizable, the potential venues and methods to impact lostness have never been more numerous.

Winning the Lost in all Cultures

Diversity, multi-cultural religions, languages, along with urbanization and technological developments, are all defining characteristics of twenty-first century North America. These factors influence the society within which both Christians and non-believers dwell side by side.

It is true that lostness is extremely personal. Every *individual* is responsible for his or her own sin, and it is the lost individual who will spend eternity separated from God. Groups of people with like interests sometimes form subcultures that focus on a particular lifestyle or religion. The nature of most subcultures is to rebel, to be non-conformist. They view Christianity, and any organized institution, as their antithesis. There are many examples of subcultures skirting the edge of our communities, but the key point is that any culture can become so devoid of God's Truth that it becomes anti-Christ and self-destructive. A society without Christ-centered governance, morals, and beliefs is bound for catastrophe. History is full of

{ EVERY BELIEVER SHARING
EVERY PERSON HEARING }

instances where empires have fallen as a result of sin.

Is there hope? Absolutely.

In God's wisdom, the Great Commission is about bringing the gospel to all peoples, and in doing so, communities are changed. Jesus came to seek and to save the lost so they might lead a purpose-filled life full of joy. In contrast, Satan's purpose is to destroy, like a thief. In Jesus' own words:

> *The thief comes only to steal and kill and destroy;*
> *I came that they may have life, and have it abundantly.*
> **JOHN 10:10**

Evangelizing the lost is nothing short of a spiritual battle. Evil is real and Satan's plans for destruction are real. Sowing the gospel, especially to those who have never been exposed to the good news, is an activity that Satan will oppose. But Paul wrote that in such opposition:

> *For our struggle is not against flesh and blood, but against the rulers,*
> *against the powers, against the world forces of this darkness.*
> **EPHESIANS 6:12**

There will be objection, hurdles, stubbornness, and rejection; yet the lost individual is not our enemy. Satan is our enemy, and those who have not accepted Jesus are blinded by him. To be victorious, believers must be committed to fight the good fight of faith and be willing to share Christ to anyone in spiritual darkness.

Are You Looking for the Lost in Your Community?

Scripture tells us that a lost person cannot see the gospel unless a Christian witnesses to that individual and God opens that person's eyes to understand it. Here, we reach the main problem: few Christians are actively *looking* for those who need a relationship with Christ and taking the light of the gospel into those dark places. Unlike Jesus' parables, many Christians are not looking for the lost sheep of North America. They cannot be found unless we search for them!

Perhaps we have difficulty in actually *seeing* the lost people around us. Too often we claim there just aren't enough hours in the day to take care of our own needs. You know the arguments: *We're too busy at work. The family takes all our attention and energy. We have too many church responsibilities already.* We conveniently believe that we have neither the time nor the expertise to get involved with the day-to-day lives of non-Christians. But Jesus, His disciples, and the early churches did exactly that. They directly connected with the daily lives of non-believers.

Jesus went where the lost lived. He walked among the people in villages and towns, and in doing so, Jesus saw and had compassion for them *"… because they were distressed and dispirited like sheep without a shepherd."*[18] Jesus saw firsthand the pain of people walking in darkness, and it moved Him to act.

Paul followed similarly when he took the gospel message from town to town and house to house. In Athens, he spent time observing all the gods that the Athenians worshipped. By taking time to study the culture, Paul's *"spirit was provoked within him as he was observing the city full of idols."*[19] Compelled, he immediately began telling the Athenians about Jesus and the power of the gospel.

The New Testament is full of the early Christians' encounters with people from all walks of life. The rich, the poor, Samaritans, lepers, an Ethiopian eunuch, slaves, beggars, fishermen, tax collectors, philosophers, Jews, Greeks, Arabians, Cretans, and others—all encountered Jesus through believers who actively shared their faith. Taking Jesus to every person, including those different from us, is not a new practice, but it has been abandoned in many areas.

{ EVERY BELIEVER SHARING }
{ EVERY PERSON HEARING }

As we strategize to get back on track evangelizing our continent, ask yourself, *who lives in my community?* Do you see the single moms struggling to take care of children while working one or two jobs? How about the homeless, the unemployed, the affluent, teachers at school, the recreational baseball team community? Do you see them as lost and in need of a Savior? What would compassion for them in the name of Christ look like as you share the gospel with them?

Maybe different kinds of people from other countries are moving into your neighborhood. Do they speak different languages? Do they dress differently and eat exotic foods? Do you see their attempts to fit into a new culture that is often difficult to understand? Trust me, they need your Christian friendship. What would compassion for them in the name of Christ look like as you share the gospel with them?

No matter where the lost people in your community are from, or their current station in life, they need to know who Jesus is and that He loves them. They are all most likely asking the same big questions: *Is there a God? Who is He? How do I find meaning in life? How do I get to know God? How will I take care of myself and those I love? What happens when I die?*

As followers of Christ, we have been given the answers to these questions and many more. You have the love of Christ in you. Will you share that love with the lost whom God has placed in your daily networks?

The outcome of searching for and finding the lost is joy. Remember Jesus' parables concerning the lost coin, sheep, and son. When the lost was found in each parable, the owners' emotions overflowed with exceeding joy. Jesus explained that in heaven:

> *...there is joy in the presence of the angels of God over one sinner who repents.*
> **LUKE 15:10**

 GPS **GOD'S PLAN** FOR **SHARING** | North America: Your Mission Field

When one sinner repents from sin and believes the gospel, there is rejoicing in heaven! The same is true today.

Christians, we have a significant amount of ground to till in order to be faithful to our Great Commission responsibilities. But the task of winning and discipling such a large population is not too big for God! We are assured by faith and in our obedience to His commands that we will see a God-sized harvest. The kingdom will expand in North America like it did in the first century.

Do you really believe that's possible?

The following chapters cover the four steps of God's Plan for Sharing: Praying, Engaging, Sowing, and Harvesting. Each section begins with an example from the mission field: stories about *real* leaders, *real* missionaries, *real* churches, *real* people, just like you, who are actively evangelizing the lost for Christ using this process. The results are amazing. I pray these examples will inspire and encourage you to find your place among them in the North American mission field.

The joy of the Lord is our strength as we begin the work of reaching our continent. Together.

{ EVERY BELIEVER SHARING }
{ EVERY PERSON HEARING }

CHAPTER TWO:
PRAYING:
Every Church Praying for Lost People

"In Canada, you can drive a thousand miles without finding an evangelical presence," says national missionary Gary Smith. Gary and his son, Caleb, were on a 12-hour road trip from Quebec to Prince Edward Island when reality hit the missionary. He started to cry. "What's going on, daddy? What's happening?" asked an alarmed Caleb. Through the tears, Gary asked his son, "Do you realize that in all of these towns, cities and villages we're passing there's no Christian church? No Sunday School classes. There's nobody telling these people about Jesus." Gary stopped the car, and he and Caleb prayed together for the towns they'd passed. It was a road trip that became a praying trip." (FIND THIS VIDEO AT NAMB VIDEO GALLERY, WWW.NAMB.NET)

The first step in God's Plan for Sharing doesn't involve walking; it involves kneeling. Prayer must be the first task in preparing for any ministry activity. God has the plan we are to follow, and with His guidance, we'll be ready.

Jesus was always prepared. He first asked the disciples to pray for helpers before preparing them with abilities and instructions to preach the gospel.[20] Christ also prepared His new church for the Holy Spirit by asking His followers to wait in Jerusalem.[21] As promised, the miracle of Pentecost—when the gospel was presented in the languages of the people assembled in Jerusalem—was the Holy Spirit's response to prayer.[22] In these instances, the result of obedience was an empowered church in which all believers witnessed with boldness.

{ EVERY BELIEVER SHARING }
{ EVERY PERSON HEARING }

Sometimes prayer is difficult for impatient believers who misunderstand it as inactive waiting. However, waiting in prayer helps us grow in our trust of how the Lord is already working.

Paul was actively waiting upon the Lord when he received the visionary Macedonian call. As a prayer-listener who was anticipating God's direction, Paul received a vision for pressing into Europe, a vision that his missionary team, comprised of Silas, Timothy, and Luke, endorsed. The missionaries were ready despite being blocked three times, but instead of retreating, Paul listened for God's direction and it was provided. Full details were not disclosed immediately, but the Lord gave exactly what was necessary to head out into the waiting harvest. God brought divine encounters, which began a movement.[23] Paul was obedient, and he was blessed.

Prayer will prepare your heart for reaching the lost and for you and your church to join God on mission.

As you develop a vision for this first step in God's Plan for Sharing, "every church praying for lost people," consider these practical aspects of praying for the lost:

1. Prepare God's People to Pray
2. Pray for the Lost
    a. Prayerwalk your community
    b. Continually discover lost people and pray for their needs
3. Pray Without Ceasing
4. Praise God Continually

Prepare God's People to Pray

Think about your friends at church. Are prayer requests centered on the unsaved? Would the guys rather talk about last night's ballgame? Would the women rather talk about their children? Or is there a concern for ways to connect with people in order to be a witness?

What about your church as a whole? Are the believers where you worship interceding for an entire group of lost people? Have there been presentations introducing church members to the spiritual needs of those in your community, state, nation, or some other place? Does your church place a premium on praying for the lost? Is it front and center?

Remember this assessment starts with *you*! The Great Commission may sound grand, but it is extremely personal. God is inviting *you* to influence *your* friends, *your* church, and even *your* own family to pray for the salvation of the lost. Every Christian is needed. Jesus told His people to *"beseech the Lord of the harvest to send out laborers into His harvest"* just before He dispatched some 35 pairs of His followers into the Judean villages where He was headed.[24] The Holy Spirit was already there, and the harvest was ready. The concern of Jesus was getting workers in the field.[25,26]

Biblical attributes are modeled by two historical workers and one current worker the Lord called to the harvest. Note that prayer was essential to their missionary work and preceded their efforts.

- Before the United States was even a country, *David Brainerd* entered a season of prayer about what God would have him do with his life. The Lord gave him a burden for Native Americans. In 1743, Brainerd was sponsored by a society in Scotland and did missionary work among Native Americans living in New York, Pennsylvania, and New Jersey. Brainerd kept a diary of his thoughts that were shaped by his intense prayer life with God. He longed to "spend and be spent for God."[27]

- *William Carey* is widely considered the father of modern missions. Before embarking on his missionary work in 1792, he described the prayer support needed for his mission work as "holding the rope." Carey knew his mentor, Andrew Fuller, was familiar with mining techniques, which in the eighteenth century required strong ropes to let the miners down into the deep, dark shafts. When prayer is "holding the rope," it becomes vital, irreplaceable, and life-

{ EVERY BELIEVER SHARING }
{ EVERY PERSON HEARING }

supporting.[28]

- *Dick May*, a North American Mission Board MSC church planting missionary in Boston, has a story to tell. And he's not shy in telling it. He says that after making contact with a co-worker of his wife in a local coffee shop, he began praying for her salvation and physical healing. Pauline Delassandra had cancer, something Dick could relate to since doctors had just told him he had a few months to live. The miracle of spiritual rebirth took place in Pauline's life due to the constant witness of the May's. The second miracle took place when, after much prayer from the church plant, Pauline was totally healed of cancer. And, in something only God could do... so was Dick. They are both now cancer free, the church is growing, and Dick is still on the streets of Boston... witnessing, praying and seeing miraculous spiritual fruit! (FIND THIS VIDEO AT **NAMB** VIDEO GALLERY, WWW.NAMB.NET)

We can trust God to prepare our hearts to do His will through our relationship with Him and by engaging in prayer. When we pray, we speak and listen, listen and speak. Once that communication link is established, prayer becomes a constant lifeline to help us conform to God's purpose.[29]

If you're like most people, you enjoy seeing the fruit, the immediate results—of evangelism. But Christ desires that we pray without becoming discouraged, even when results are not forthcoming. As an example of persistence in prayer, Jesus tells a parable in Luke 18:1-8 about the unrighteous judge and the widow who nagged him until he finally agreed to her request. The Syrophoenician woman's plea for even the *"crumbs"* from Jesus to cast the demon from her vexed daughter is another example of using fortitude in our prayer encounters with the Lord.[30]

Pray for the Lost

> *To say that 'prayer changes things' is not as close to the truth as saying, 'Prayer changes me and then I change things.' God has established things so that prayer, on the basis of redemption, changes the way a person looks at things.*
>
> OSWALD CHAMBERS [31]

When was the last time you actually wept over a lost person's need for salvation? When have you grieved over entire people groups who have yet to hear God's message of salvation? The lost desperately need prayers—*your* prayers—lifted up on their behalf. A simple reminder, such as a memento, a photo, or prayer card, reminds us to pray even when we're distracted by other life activities.

If you've ever been around a group of Korean believers in North America, you certainly know what it means to be fervent in prayer! Many Korean believers often start their prayer meetings before dawn. For these faithful believers, sleep can be sacrificed when one soul has yet to hear, or when one worker has yet to be prayed into the harvest. I have personally found the "Who's in Your Wallet?" prayer card helpful. The size of a credit card, it provides a place for you to pray for three lost people by name. Having these names of the lost people in my wallet reminds me to pray for them every time I take out a credit card, and it prompts me to find ways to share with them.

Dedicated times of prayer help us renew our mind and commitment to the Lord. In our modern day, Rees Howell was a man who sacrificed his health in order to pray for the lost around him, often into the night. Howell worked as a miner, but through his concentrated prayer life, he saw revivals break out across Great Britain and South Africa.[32]

{ EVERY BELIEVER SHARING }
{ EVERY PERSON HEARING }

Praying John Hyde was a missionary to India who also spent many hours praying through the night. He formed the Punjab Prayer Union and began praying that one person would be saved every day. This was unheard of in 1900. Yet, God moved, and the people responded as 400 were baptized in one year.[33] The next year, he led them to double their goal, and more than 800 were baptized!

In Acts 7, we read about the stoning of Stephen and how he stayed in riveted contact with Jesus to the very end of his earth-bound life. His walk with the Lord was such that crossing over into Jesus' arms was merely an unbroken continuation. And yet, in the midst of a hail of stones, Stephen was able to repeat the words of Jesus (see Acts 7:59-60). He prayed for his accusers and their murderous actions against him. Jesus' act of forgiveness on the cross, and Stephen's forgiveness of his attackers, had a strong impact on believers in the early church.

> *Prayer brings the omnipotent God of the universe into the struggle of rescuing souls from Satan's kingdom and transferring them into Jesus' kingdom.*[34]
>
> EVELYN CHRISTENSEN

Jesus taught His disciples to pray for the kingdom of God to come on earth. As pastor and theologian John Piper pointed out, *"Hallowed be thy name. Thy kingdom come ... is a missionary prayer."*[35] When our prayer aligns with Jesus' model, our relationship with the Father is strengthened. God clearly invites us to be His instruments of peace, and to bring reverence to His name. When we are obedient and compassionate, the kingdom of God can spread throughout all peoples in North America.

Paul was the epitome of a compassionate prayer warrior. He urged everyone to not only put on the full armor of God, but also *"with all prayer and petition pray at all times in the Spirit, and with this in view, be on the alert with all perseverance and petition for all the saints."*[36] He also pointed to prayer as the supply source for missionary workers and the expansion of the gospel:

> *Finally, brethren, pray for us that the word of the Lord will*
> *spread rapidly and be glorified, just as it did also with you.*
> **2 THESSALONIANS 3:1**

Paul had a big vision for the good news of Christ. Even though the mission field was full of stony hearts, Paul persisted, not out of duty, but out of love. When Paul wrote to the church in Rome, he expressed deep anguish over the Jews who had rejected Jesus as Lord and Messiah:

> *I am telling the truth in Christ, I am not lying, my conscience*
> *testifies with me in the Holy Spirit, that I have great sorrow and*
> *unceasing grief in my heart. For I could wish that I myself were accursed,*
> *separated from Christ for the sake of my brethren, my kinsmen*
> *according to the flesh.*
> **ROMANS 9:1-3**

Paul's heart broke for the lost. Can we say the same thing?

Prayerwalk Your Community

Prayerwalking is an effective way to gain insight from God about how to pray for the people in your area. The next time you take your dog for a walk through the neighborhood, simply pray as you pass by the homes along your street. If you see toys in the front yard of a house, you know that children live there. Pray specifically for those children to be nurtured so that they will come to know Jesus at an early age. Pray for the parents to be influenced by godly people and to seek Jesus as their Lord and Savior.

{ EVERY BELIEVER SHARING }
{ EVERY PERSON HEARING }

Being a consistent prayerwalker may also provide opportunities for you to interact with those for whom you are praying. As God brings divine encounters, let people know you are praying for the area and ask how you can pray for them. The Holy Spirit will help you discern their spiritual condition by how they respond. As you talk with them, look for ways to ask if they know Jesus, and be ready to share the plan of salvation or pray with them on the spot if they are willing.

Years ago, while working in Montgomery, Ala., Neal Hughes, now with the North American Mission Board, led his church to prayerwalk several gated communities and multihousing units where little, if any, evangelizing had preceded them. The seven-week plan, called "The Jericho Prayer Walk," resulted in the formation of several small-group Bible studies. Those Bible study groups then grew into new churches! Neal explained:

> *When prayerwalking, I am praying the resurrected Christ through those locked doors. Jesus wants to announce peace to them. They become overjoyed when discovering the Lord!*[37]

Prayerwalkers can be trained and mobilized through churches and associations to cover every street and person within a community. Excellent resources are available to equip potential prayerwalkers such as *"Taking Prayer to the Streets,"* (This and other resources mentioned can be found in the Additional Recommended Resources at the end of this book.) which includes methods of involving those who stay and pray at the church as well as those who go into the community.

Continually Discover Lost People and Pray for Their Needs

One way to continually discover lost people is to heighten our awareness of the people who live around us. You and I drive by the same houses every day on the way home from the office or from running errands. Do we know the people who live there? Do we know the neighbor to our left, to our right, or across the street? Do they know Jesus?

Informed praying for the lost is foundational to God's Plan for Sharing. Jesus pointed out that He could *"do nothing of Himself, unless it is something He sees the Father doing; for whatever the Father does, these things the Son also does in like manner."*[38]

If we actively wait upon and listen for the Lord, He will let us know who, among the people we see every day, needs salvation. Someone you encounter may be a modern-day Moses who, at least on the surface, seems to have no redeeming value. But God sees that individual's potential to impact an entire group. These individuals are often those "persons of peace" whom Jesus described in Luke 10:6 who can open doors of faith among others in their networks.

God was fully prepared to wipe out Israel because of their sin, but Moses changed His heart through prayer:

> *Turn from Your burning anger and change Your mind about doing harm to Your people. Remember Abraham, Isaac, and Israel, Your servants to whom You swore by Yourself, and said to them, 'I will multiply your descendants as the stars of the heavens, and all this land of which I have spoken I will give to your descendants, and they shall inherit it forever.'*
> *So the LORD changed His mind about the harm which He said He would do to His people.*
> EXODUS 32:12B-14

One prayer can save many people!

A woman in Alabama once received a Bible in Farsi and began praying for someone special to whom she could give it. While praying, she realized her daughter was playing with her next door friend. Out of curiosity, the woman asked the playmate, *"What language do you speak at home?"* The little girl smiled and said, *"Farsi. We're from Iran."* Wow! The visit with the mother next door went very well, and the Bible was given to the family. Prayer enabled a relationship that led to an active witness. Who knows

{ EVERY BELIEVER SHARING }
{ EVERY PERSON HEARING }

how far that Iranian family may take the gospel?

The harvest fields of twenty-first century North America are filled with diverse and changing populations. Christ encountered all types of people in His day: religious sects (Pharisees, Sadducees), people in need (lepers, the blind, the lame), and occupational groups (fishermen, tax collectors, scribes, teachers, soldiers). Christ never flinched at their sin or differences. He saw only their hearts. Likewise, God provides the confidence we need to reach the people He places before us. Author Minette Drumwright explained it this way:

> *God has chosen to accomplish His purposes in this world in response to the prayers of His people. This is His strategy: He releases power as His people pray. He combines our strategic prayers and His power to make a difference in the flow of the gospel into remote and difficult places of the world, as well as those peoples and places close at hand. He graciously gives us this essential role of partnership with Him.*[39]

When we walk with the Lord, He teaches us how to love groups of people enough to intercede for them. As our will conforms to His concern for a lost world, the results will amaze us!

Does your heart break for a lost person or an entire lost group of people? Do you, like Moses, stammer out, *"Who am I to help them?"* Or, do you step up and plead in fervent prayer, *"Lord, please do not destroy them, but save these people"?*

Pray Without Ceasing

Chuck Lawless is the dean of the Billy Graham School of Missions, Evangelism and Church Growth. On the suggestion that prayer precede ministry, Chuck agreed:

> *Actually, the Bible assumes that we will pray.... Prayer was nonnegotiable in the life of [the early] church—as it should be in today's church. God expects us to pray, and He expects us to grow healthy churches that focus on praying.*[40]

Recognize that prayer is not only a part of worship, but also the foundation for our evangelistic efforts among the unreached of North America. When we approach the throne of God with humility, knowing He is in control of every outcome, we become active participants in His mission. You and I achieve nothing on our own:

> *Therefore, we are ambassadors for Christ, as though God were making an appeal through us; we beg you on behalf of Christ, be reconciled to God.*
>
> **2 CORINTHIANS 5:20**

Only through God's involvement, which we evoke through prayer, will we be ready to take to the fields and begin working with the soil to prepare it for the gospel.

I encourage you to stop now and pray for the lost people in your life and in your community. Then head into the field. It's time to engage with them as a witness.

Praise God Continually

Praising God is the activity of heaven. Even in The Lord's Prayer, praise is the first order of business. Praise should be part of our focus as we grow

{ EVERY BELIEVER SHARING }
{ EVERY PERSON HEARING }

in the awareness of God's will for our lives.[41] A spirit of gratitude and thanksgiving for the new insights God gives us deepens our concern for the lost and increases our desire to pray.

> *All Your works shall give thanks to You, O LORD, And Your godly ones shall bless You. They shall speak of the glory of Your kingdom, And talk of Your power; To make known to the sons of men mighty acts, And the glory of the majesty of Your kingdom.*
> **PSALM 145:10-12**

North America is blessed with physical wealth and political freedom. We have so much to be thankful for; yet we take God for granted, expecting more, rather than being grateful and content with His blessings. What arrogance we demonstrate when we do not give the glory to God for the great things He does. We know He is faithful just by seeing the consistency of the sun rising and setting every day with majestic beauty. What a creative God we serve!

Praise needs to happen even before we begin sowing down the gospel and reaping a harvest. We can praise God for going ahead of us into the field and laying the groundwork for our involvement.

God is worthy of our praise, and we get to know Him by praising Him for who He is. Praise God when He shows us a lost person whom we had overlooked before. Praise Him when that person begins to show interest in spiritual things. And of course, praise God for saving that person.

When we tell someone about Jesus, we are praising Him. We are sharing how great He is, how much He loves us, and what He has done in our lives. The more we get to know Jesus personally, the more we want to praise Him as a way of life. As the old hymn says, *"O for a thousand tongues to sing the praises of our God and King!"*[42]

CHAPTER THREE:
ENGAGING:
Every Believer Sharing as a
Trained Witness

No matter where you find him, Ken Dean, a missionary in Los Angeles, is engaging with the lost, or teaching pastors and churches how to engage their mission field. Ken knows his field well; he's worked with the city on gang prevention, and because of his consistent witness, gang members are now former gang members—and Christians. "I'm just doing what Jesus taught us to do by His example. Getting out in and among the people," he explained. Ken believes that you can't effectively take the saving, healing power of the gospel to people until you get outside the four walls of the church and engage the community. Whether it's through a meals program, prison ministry, or after-school tutoring, there is a mission field outside your church that needs to hear about Jesus. (FIND THIS VIDEO AT NAMB VIDEO GALLERY, WWW. NAMB.NET)

No farmer ends his workday as clean as he began that morning. His clothes will be filthy and sweaty. Earth will be rubbed into his hands. His skin will be baked from the sun. Readying a field for planting requires the farmer to interact with the soil, plowing the dirt, and removing stones so seeds can grow and flourish. The farmer must engage with the land being cultivated. It may seem like unpleasant work, but the farmer knows the effort will be rewarded with an abundant crop, which brings great joy.

In the same way, engaging with non-believers is a vital part of God's Plan for Sharing so that everyone can hear the gospel. Engaging means participating and being actively involved in the enterprise of witnessing and reaching people for Christ. When we are equipped, trained, and ready

{ EVERY BELIEVER SHARING }
{ EVERY PERSON HEARING }

as witnesses, Christ gives us everything we need to transform the world. We won't go alone. The Lord promises to send His presence and power ahead of us and with us. Without engaging, there will be no real sowing and no harvesting. Without engaging, North America will not hear the gospel, and the future will be no different than it is now.

Jesus went straight to the people who needed Him most, even if doing so went against popular culture. In John 4 we read about Jesus' travels from Judea to Galilee by way of Samaria. No decent Jew went through Samaria. The Jews hated the mixed-race people there and would actually travel farther to avoid going through Samaria. But Jesus led His disciples directly through that land and to the woman at the well. He engaged her in a conversation about her life, her beliefs, and her sin. He offered her Living Water: Himself.

The Great Commission is all about engaging, interacting and building relationships with lost people. The early church understood this and literally transformed their world. All four Gospels and the book of Acts contain the charge to evangelize. Jesus told each believer to go into the world to make disciples, which includes sharing the good news with others. Paul wrote: *"faith comes from hearing, and hearing by the word of Christ."*[43]   Realizing that people must first hear the Word in order to respond, Paul asked:

> *How will they believe in Him whom they have not heard?*
> *And how will they hear without a preacher? How will they preach*
> *unless they are sent? Just as it is written, "How beautiful are the feet of*
> *those who bring good news of good things!"*
> **ROMANS 10:14B-15**

Silent Believers

How can anyone who has been redeemed by the blood of Christ keep quiet about it? If we know about an excellent new restaurant or television program, we don't hesitate to tell everyone we know about it. The key to eternal salvation is in our heart; yet so many of us keep silent. Why?

When believers are asked why they don't share their faith, there are several responses. Some think that unless they are living perfect lives, they are not worthy to witness. Although living a life that honors Christ is important in effective witnessing, no one is perfect. Paul himself shared that he was the *"chief among sinners"* (see 1 Timothy 1:15). If Paul considered himself worthy to share the gospel of Christ, then certainly we have no excuse! Being transparent and open to personal struggles of imperfection and how Christ has made a difference can be a powerful testimony. It communicates authenticity.

Another response is an unrealistic understanding of what it means to be a "successful" witness. Some ask: *What if the person to whom I witness does not receive Christ? What if I mess up the gospel presentation and the person walks away more confused?* Each of us must understand that we are not responsible for the results. In the book, *People Sharing Jesus*, author Darrell Robinson noted, *"Our job is to share; God's job is to bring results."*[44] A successful witness is simply one who shares. It is one who obeys the command of God to go and tell. This understanding reduces the pressure and gives us freedom to leave the responses to God.

Universalism has become a prominent cultural issue that also keeps believers from seeing the need to witness. This point of view espouses that Jesus is just one of many ways to "get to heaven." He is not the only way, and He is not unique. Jesus refuted this opinion, saying:

> *I am the way, and the truth, and the life;*
> *no one comes to the Father, but through Me.*
> **JOHN 14:6**

{ EVERY BELIEVER SHARING }
{ EVERY PERSON HEARING }

This theological truth cannot be watered down. It is either true or false. To deny its credibility is to deny the authority of the Scripture and the words of Christ. If this truth is compromised, then the implication is that Jesus is a liar. If Jesus is a liar, then salvation does not exist.

One of the most cited reasons many believers do not witness is fear, which is shown in a variety of ways. First, there may be the fear of rejection. In a witnessing experience, it is important to understand that a hard-hearted person is rejecting Jesus, not the person sharing. Believers cannot control the results, only the activity of sharing. Jesus was rejected by His own people, but that didn't discourage Him from fulfilling His mission and message.

Not knowing *how* to witness may be connected to a fear of witnessing. According to the Bible, the gospel is so simple that even a child can understand it. Still, many believers feel that becoming trained in sharing the gospel will be difficult and time-consuming. This assumption is simply incorrect. Many witness training resources can help believers at all spiritual levels get beyond this fear and into the field.

The prerequisite to sharing the gospel is a heart for the lost.

Fear and faith cannot coexist. Fear is a stumbling block and an enemy to sharing Christ. Satan himself would love to keep believers from becoming trained witnesses. His goal is to discourage us and rob us of the joy of salvation. He wants us to question our faith and our worth before God. His desire is to destroy the plan of God and create apathy among believers that will paralyze effective evangelism. But remember we are made more than conquerors. By putting on the full armor of God as Paul instructed in Ephesians 6:10-18, we can stand against Satan's schemes. We are made strong in the Lord and in His mighty power.

Preparing Witnesses for the Field

So, how do believers become trained witnesses? In general, the gospel contains five primary points. First, God created us and loves us. Second, we have a sin problem. Third, God sent the gift of His Son Jesus to pay the penalty for our sin on the cross and to offer us forgiveness. Fourth, God wants us to respond in repentance and faith and receive Jesus as our personal Lord and Savior. Last, as a result, He gives us life now and forever. Nothing could be more simple! When Jesus spoke to the Samaritan woman at the well, He used this basic format.[45] He gently guided her to acknowledge her sin of adultery, offered her a solution through forgiveness, and lovingly assured her of eternal life.

What happened next? The Samaritan woman went into the town and told everyone what had happened to her.

One of the most effective ways to share the good news of the gospel is by telling your story. You don't need a seminary degree or a PhD. Every believer already has the necessary tool. It is your personal testimony, the story of your encounter with Christ and how He has transformed your life. A personal testimony cannot be refuted since it is your experience. It is powerful and communicates to others the impact Christ has made on your life.

A personal story or testimony contains four areas:

1. **The first area communicates your life *before* you made a commitment to follow Jesus.** What was going on? What was it like before you received Jesus? You may have been struggling with drugs, alcohol, loneliness, or lack of purpose. You may have been unhappy and unfulfilled. Whatever it may have been, it is your story. Maybe you were a child when you accepted Christ, but experienced a defining moment as an adult that clearly confirmed your salvation.

2. **Second, a personal story communicates *how* you received Christ as your personal Lord and Savior.** Where were you? When was it?

{ EVERY BELIEVER SHARING }
{ EVERY PERSON HEARING }

Maybe you were in a church service and responded to an invitation. Perhaps you were at a Christian camp or attending vacation Bible school when you asked Jesus into your heart. It could have resulted from a conversation with a friend, family member, or work associate who shared Christ and you responded. Whenever it happened, that day became your "spiritual" birthday, the day you became a newborn "babe in Christ."

3. **A personal story gives you a chance to communicate *what* you understood about the gospel when you received Christ as your personal Savior.** This gives you a chance to explain the essential content of the gospel that we mentioned earlier. Here is a good place to use some simple illustrations and ask some questions to make sure the listener understands what you are saying. As we explain the gospel, the Holy Spirit is at work in the life of the hearer, convincing him/her of sin and the need for forgiveness.[46]

4. **Last, your personal story communicates how your life has been *changed* since you received Christ.** Most of us could write a book on what He has done in our lives. Salvation is transforming, and we all have stories of how our old lives passed away as we became new creations in Christ.

Christians can be equipped in many ways to share the gospel with unbelievers. Ideally, every church provides witness training classes and workshops. Dozens of resources are available through which believers can learn to effectively share the truths of the gospel. The North American Mission Board, along with LifeWay Christian Resources, provides materials ranging from simple one-hour or one-day training workshops[47] to a more in-depth witness preparedness study called *The NET*.[48]

If your church does not yet offer classes on how to share the gospel, then by all means, seek out a resource and teach it! When you do, your church becomes more involved and motivated to leave its comfort zone and venture out into the fields that are ripe for harvest. Nothing can excite and revolutionize the body of Christ more than seeing new Christians publically professing their faith through baptism.

Imagine how our culture would change if every believer shared the gospel as they went about their day. No doubt the world would be turned upside down just like it was in the book of Acts. People would be changed; lives would be transformed. New churches would spring up, and believers would live with a passion for the lost that overflows from an intimate walk with God.

If we are to fulfill the Great Commission, we must take personal responsibility for sharing Christ in our own Jerusalem—across the street, around the block, to friends, coworkers and family. Some of us will stay in our communities, and others may be called to cross significant geographical or cultural barriers to share Christ as short or long-term missionaries. Regardless of the location, the challenge is the same.

Are you ready to personally engage in sharing your faith, and are you preparing workers to go into the field and sow the gospel among all people?

{ EVERY BELIEVER SHARING }
{ EVERY PERSON HEARING }

CHAPTER FOUR:
SOWING:
Every Lost Person Receiving a Witness

"This is the best group of people I could pastor. These are my heroes," said military chaplain Jeff Struecker, who himself has seen every front line of battle since Panama. "The Army has a tendency to confront people with who they are physically, mentally and spiritually. The more difficult the circumstances, the more receptive the average person becomes to issues of faith and spiritual matters. I have the opportunity to help them grow spiritually as they undergo these harsh conditions." In one year, Struecker led more than 30 Ranger cadets to Christ in Ft. Benning, Ga. Most of these soldiers have already been in combat. And the ones that haven't will soon be deployed to Iraq and Afghanistan. He takes every opportunity to sow down the Gospel. "There's a very real urgency for me to share the gospel of Jesus Christ," he said. (FIND THIS VIDEO AT NAMB VIDEO GALLERY, WWW.NAMB.NET)

Jesus said a lot about sowing. It was among His favorite metaphors for teaching spiritual truths to a primarily agrarian society. The farming people of His day understood the concepts of preparing soil and nurturing seeds in order to obtain a great harvest, and they could relate Jesus' stories to the principles He was explaining to them about the kingdom of God.

{ EVERY BELIEVER SHARING
EVERY PERSON HEARING }

Perhaps Christ's best known parable about sowing is found in Matthew 13 where the gospel represents a seed sown on a variety of soils.

> *Behold, the sower went out to sow; and as he sowed,*
> *some seeds fell beside the road, and the birds came and ate them up.*
> *Others fell on the rocky places, where they did not have much soil;*
> *and immediately they sprang up, because they had no depth of soil...*
> *Others fell among the thorns, and the thorns came up and*
> *choked them out. And others fell on the good soil and yielded a crop,*
> *some a hundredfold...*
> **Matthew 13:3b-8a**

Even today, when the majority of North Americans live in cities, this story paints a powerful picture of the challenge that lies before witnessing believers. Each lost person's heart is unique. Some are fertile and ready to hear about Jesus. Others are hard and bitter toward God.

Early in Jesus' ministry, He talked with His disciples about several basic principles of sowing and harvesting. His teaching set the stage for what He wanted the disciples to know as they prepared to follow Him.

> *My food is to do the will of Him who sent Me and to accomplish*
> *His work. Do you not say, "There are yet four months,*
> *and then comes the harvest?" Behold, I say to you, lift up your eyes*
> *and look on the fields, that they are white for harvest. Already he*
> *who reaps is receiving wages and is gathering fruit for life eternal;*
> *so that he who sows and he who reaps may rejoice together. For in this*
> *case the saying is true, "One sows and another reaps." I sent you to*
> *reap that for which you have not labored; others have labored and*
> *you have entered into their labor.*
> **John 4:34-38**

Clearly Jesus was challenging his disciples with a sense of urgency. But our fields are ripe today as well. People are living and dying without Christ every day. Whose responsibility is it to share the gospel with them? It is your responsibility, and it is my responsibility.

Sow Down North America with the Gospel

When it comes to spiritual things, all of us love to harvest. We love to share the gospel and see someone pray to receive Jesus as Lord and Savior. It's even more exciting when these two activities happen very close together. We strike up a conversation with someone, God opens an opportunity to share the gospel, and we get to witness the conversion of that person. Most of the time, we walk away thinking that God allowed us to handle the entire process. However, in almost every case, someone else has been involved in sowing the gospel in that person's life. Perhaps a parent has been praying for that individual. Maybe another Christian has been a faithful witness, or a pastor has ministered to that person in a time of hurt or crisis. Others have been sowing long before we arrived and were able to actually "harvest" the new believer for the kingdom.

The ground is not always so fertile. Sometimes we plant in an unsown, or lightly sown, mission field. North America is now home to many people who have little or no exposure to Christianity. All around us are people who have not had the gospel intentionally sown among them.

In previous chapters, we've discussed the population tapestry of North America in all its complex, yet rich, diversity. In Chapter 1, I mentioned a census statistic that you may have found surprising: nearly 50 percent of the U.S. population will be comprised of an ethnicity other than Caucasian by 2050. That seems far off in the future, but we are already noticing the astounding growth of Muslims, Hindus, Buddhists, and other non-Christian groups who bring with them a culture and worldview that challenge the church in fulfilling the Great Commission. To reach

{ EVERY BELIEVER SHARING }
{ EVERY PERSON HEARING }

this increasingly diverse and generally non-Christian population, we need to do lots of sowing. One of our tasks, then, is to ensure that all the people groups in North America have a chance to hear the gospel in their language.

Several truths help guide our gospel-sowing activity. First, realize that we sow in areas where others will reap. Second, and the flip side of the coin, is that we will reap where others have sown. Jesus clearly stated this in John 4:38 when He told the disciples, *"I have sent you to reap that for which you have not labored..."* If you have led people to Christ, you have most likely been the recipient of someone else's sowing. Even Paul acknowledged this when he wrote:

> *I planted, Apollos watered, but God was causing the growth.*
> *So then neither the one who plants nor the one who waters is anything,*
> *but God who causes the growth. Now he who plants and he who waters*
> *are one; but each will receive his own reward according to his own labor.*
> *For we are God's fellow workers; you are God's field, God's building.*
> **I Corinthians 3:6-9**

Praise the Lord for this!

Finally, we reap *after* we have sown. There is always some gap between sowing and reaping. For some people, it's just moments; for others, it takes years. In either case, the harvest of just one person makes all the effort worthwhile.

We Must Sow in Order to Reap

Aside from the occasional wild berries or volunteer plant, rarely do we get to harvest something edible and usable without deliberately planting. Anyone who has ever tried to grow a vegetable garden understands this. Therefore, if the relationship of sowing and harvesting is apparent when talking about a physical seed, then why do we think we can harvest spiritually without first sowing the gospel seed?

Sowing the gospel is hard work. We may find ourselves in fields that are not well-cultivated, full of weeds, or appear a bit hostile to us as the sower. So, if the situation seems too uncomfortable, we may choose not to sow, waiting instead until the crops are ripe for picking. But as the natural law of sowing and harvesting cannot be avoided, neither can the spiritual law. We will not ever harvest if we have not been intentional about sowing—*somewhere*. Remember, the field we reap may not be the field we have sown.

You and I don't have to look far to find a field in which to sow. North America is full of communities that need to hear the good news. As Christians, we are commanded to make disciples of all people, providing them an opportunity to hear, understand and respond to the gospel message in their cultural context.[49] Recall that our job is to sow the gospel seed, not to bring about conversion. That is the work of the Holy Spirit in the lives of those who receive the message.[50]

Many believers witness best among the established relationships they have built at home, play and work. Often the biggest hindrance to our witness is fear of rejection; yet, statistics demonstrate that 78 percent of non-Christians in North America say they would be willing to listen to someone who wanted to share the gospel with them.[51] People today are open to a discussion about spiritual matters, and in many instances, they are actively seeking direction.

Sow in Prepared Fields

A future harvest requires sowing today, and part of effective sowing means preparing the field. Two great passages of Scripture illustrate this. One is found in the passage mentioned earlier in John 4 where Jesus reminded the disciples they are reaping in areas where others have worked.

{ EVERY BELIEVER SHARING
EVERY PERSON HEARING }

In the NIV translation, the passage reads:

> *I sent you to reap what you have not worked for. Others have done the hard work, and you have reaped the benefits of their labor.*
> JOHN 4:38 (NIV)

Notice the three words describing what sowers do: "work," "hard work," and "labor." How I wish Jesus didn't describe the task of gospel sowing using these kinds of words! Each of these terms indicate that sowing is work, and hard work at that. Just look at an uncultivated field or the flower pot on your porch that still contains last year's weeds. Getting a field ready to plant is labor-intensive, just as preparing a person or group of people to hear the gospel is hard work. Studies indicate that in today's multicultural and fast-paced society, 50-60 repeated contacts with a non-believer are required to win that person to Christ.[52] That's a lot of sowing!

Look once again at Jesus' parable of the sower. This passage is filled with images of unprepared soil and hard work. As the sower went along, he scattered seed everywhere. Some fell on the hard, beaten-down dirt path that was inhospitable to seeds and easy for the birds to find. Other seeds fell on rocky ground where the seeds sprouted quickly, but lacked enough dirt to grow good roots. Still other seeds fell in places where there was competition with weeds and thorns. Some found good ground, soil that was prepared and ready for the seed. The result was an abundant harvest—thirty, sixty and one hundred times the seed that was originally scattered. This is what we are looking for in North America—prepared soil where the seed of the gospel can take deep root and produce an abundant harvest!

There are many ways to prepare the "soil" in your community. You can impact the growing multi-cultural population by simply dining at restaurants owned and frequented by people of an ethnicity different from your own. Get to know the owner as well as regulars that stop by. Prayerwalk or drive an international neighborhood regularly. Take advantage of opportunities to stop and interact with people in the market, restaurants and other public areas. As part of your church's ministry, take a welcome basket to a new family in your neighborhood or host an international student in your home during the holidays. In all of these scenarios, you are sharing the love of Christ. Even when language seems to separate us, a simple act of kindness will open doors to plant the gospel seed. Teaching English as a second language is a great way to get to know internationals and share the gospel.

A cookie-cutter approach to evangelism and church planting is no longer effective. If we are going to have an impact in North America and our own backyard, we must seek to understand our neighbors and contextualize the presentation of the gospel for them. The gospel message does not change, but rather, the way we present it in order to bridge the gap created by culture, language and worldview may change.

Think outside the box, beyond the ways we've always done evangelism. Creative opportunities for contextualizing the gospel to the lost in your community are infinite. Present the plan of salvation during a music festival or cultural event in the native language of an ethnic community, or become familiar with other world religions so you can highlight the unique assurance of salvation that only Christ brings. Or, share the gospel in a venue that allows your church to meet the physical needs of a group. The object is simply to engage with people *where they are*. This is the hard work of preparing people to receive the gospel!

You Will Reap as You Sow

Ever notice how one seed can produce a harvest that is exponentially larger than itself? This is an amazing law of nature! For example, imagine a farmer goes out and plants one kernel of corn in his field. He has prepared the soil and done everything he can for that kernel of corn to grow into a tall, healthy corn stalk. As he works, he keeps the soil loose, removes the weeds, sprays to kill any insects that might attack the plant, fertilizes to

{ EVERY BELIEVER SHARING
EVERY PERSON HEARING }

add nutrients, and irrigates the field to provide necessary moisture.

The farmer has little control over the sun and weather conditions, but he does everything else in his power to help that seed germinate and grow into a mature stalk. Along the way, two or three cobs begin to form. As they continue to grow and develop, rows of kernels form along each cob until there are literally hundreds of kernels. Multiply that by two or three ears of corn on a single stalk, and the farmer now has a bountiful harvest, all initiated by that one tiny kernel.

There are two applications of this principle. First, the more you sow, the more you will harvest:

> *Now this I say, he who sows sparingly will also reap sparingly, and he who sows bountifully will also reap bountifully.*
> **2 Corinthians 9:6**

Paul used these words to teach the Corinthians about giving, but the principle applies to gospel sowing as well. Do you want an abundant harvest? Sow generously. Sow sparingly, and be prepared for a meager harvest.

The second principle is one of great blessing. Just like the one kernel of corn that can produce hundreds of kernels, our gospel sowing among one group of people can bring hundreds of people into the kingdom. Our sowing of the gospel seed, planted in the life of the right person, can multiply many times over. The Samaritan woman told many people about her encounter with Christ at the well. Despite her reputation, people were curious about her story. They wanted to see for themselves. The Bible says that many from the village believed in Jesus on that day. The single seed was multiplied many times over!

Sowing in Tears: Reap in Joy

In the Old Testament, David closed one of his songs with a great promise for those of us who are committed to sowing the gospel among all people groups in North America:

> *Those who sow in tears shall reap with joyful shouting. He who goes to and fro weeping, carrying his bag of seed, shall indeed come again with a shout of joy, bringing his sheaves with him.*
> **PSALM 126:5-6**

Sheaves are large bundles of wheat or corn stalks, the end result of careful planting and an abundant harvest. What an awesome promise from God! If we sow with tears of grief, burdened over the lostness of North America, God promises that we will also reap with songs of joy. We go out to sow seeds, but return with blessings. It's a win-win situation. Everyone receives a blessing—the new believer *and* the sower!

We live in a culture that is perhaps more like the first century in which the gospel was initially proclaimed, than any of the previous twenty centuries. It is a culture that grows more pluralistic and secular every day, with expanding pockets throughout North America where the gospel is not always welcome.

Yet, we have been called to this specific time and place for a reason. It's no coincidence. We are Christ's ambassadors in the country, town and neighborhood where God has brought us. By living out our faith in the midst of our relationships, through acts of kindness, and verbally sowing the gospel, we connect with a lost world and help bring about the transformation of our communities.

The apostle Paul declared in his letter to the Romans:

{ EVERY BELIEVER SHARING }
{ EVERY PERSON HEARING }

For I am not ashamed of the gospel, for it is the power of God for salvation to everyone who believes, to the Jew first and also to the Greek.
ROMANS 1:16

Paul never forgot what the resurrected Christ did for him on the road to Damascus.[53] He never took his decision to become a follower of Christ lightly. Paul was not ashamed. As a result, he lived his life in such a way that the love of Christ flowed from him into those of every country he visited. If Paul's life was marked by anything, it was marked by his passion to sow the gospel among those who had not yet heard.

Are you interested in reaping an abundant harvest in your area? Then may we be like Paul in doing everything we can to see that the gospel is abundantly sown among every person and people group in North America. An abundant harvest is waiting!

CHAPTER FIVE:
HARVESTING:
Every Church Harvesting and Celebrating Every Salvation Response

Jeff Smith is not your everyday Baptist preacher. In fact, every Sunday he looks like he's ready for a rodeo, and for Jeff, that's probably just about right. Jeff was called to start a cowboy church a number of years ago, which he did. But it didn't stop there. From that one church, his team has planted dozens of other cowboy churches and hundreds, maybe even thousands, have come to Christ because of it. One thing Jeff loves is celebrating when a soul comes to Christ. These new believers get on the back of a pickup truck, are driven into the riding rink (where the church meets), and then walk into an eight-foot long trough filled with water for baptism. When that new believer comes back up out of the water, the congregation erupts into applause, tears and laughter—a real celebration. (FIND THIS VIDEO AT NAMB VIDEO GALLERY, WWW.NAMB.NET)

Last words are lasting words. That's why Jesus waited until His post-resurrection ministry to share the Great Commission with His disciples. He wanted them to remember this assignment. While harvesting is not more important than the other aspects of God's Plan for Sharing, the entire process crumbles without proper harvesting. Our corn farmer would shudder at the idea of leaving a crop that he had so carefully planted and tended, to spoil in the field! He would bring in as many helpers as possible to assist him in picking the crop quickly, before it is lost. And yet harvesting, especially through public events, has fallen on hard times among Southern Baptists. We're leaving a ripe harvest of potential believers in the field.

{ EVERY BELIEVER SHARING
EVERY PERSON HEARING }

Thus far in *God's Plan for Sharing*, we have discussed the following principles:

- **Praying:** Every church praying for every lost person,
- **Engaging:** Every believer sharing as a trained witness, and
- **Sowing:** Every lost person receiving a witness.

Now the final piece of the plan:

- **Harvesting:** Every church harvesting and celebrating every salvation response.

If you've ever observed surfing fanatics, whether in the Gulf of Mexico or along the west coast, a universal truth about the sport emerges: surfers never *create* waves, they just catch them. Likewise, we don't create the waves of God's Spirit, we just catch them. *Is God still sending the waves of His Spirit through harvest events?* Many church growth conferences over the past ten years have broadcast the notion that "event evangelism"—preaching the gospel during a publicized community activity or event—is a thing of the past. However, harvest events are biblical, and overwhelmingly, churches that are reaching and baptizing a large number of lost people are riding the wave of harvest events in small groups or large events.

As you set out to begin harvesting, I encourage you to consider a few strategies that have been effective in spreading the gospel in other areas of North America:

- Hosting intentionally-evangelistic events
- Following up with and assimilating new believers
- Celebrating believers' baptism, and
- Starting something new in ministry

I believe these ministry characteristics result in the most fruitful harvests within our twenty-first century culture.

Host Intentional Harvest Events

Early on in the book of Acts, Luke provided a strategy for reaching people that is still applicable today. He recorded how the early church obeyed the Great Commission by leaving the prayer room and intentionally sharing the gospel of Jesus Christ on the day of Pentecost, taking advantage of the amazing spectacle that God provided to attract attention. The event described in Acts 1 and 2 is a model for our harvest event strategies, and it's as simple as A-B-C:

- **A = Attraction.** Pentecost was an astounding display! There was a supernatural voice (God), a violent wind, fireworks (tongues of fire), and a recitation of the languages of the world. What a commotion! Just imagine 120 Galileans speaking languages they had never learned! The event captured the attention of the city. The people wanted to know what was going on.[54]
- **B = Bridges.** The disciples' response to Christ was one of obedience and dependence on God. In obedience, before Pentecost, they waited and prayed. According to Acts 1:14, they *"were continually devoting themselves to prayer."* Shortly thereafter, the Holy Spirit came with power and transformation, and the disciples obediently shared. The vertical bridge is the great prayer movement of the early church, while the horizontal bridge is people reaching people. After Pentecost, the disciples and spectators went out into the city and told what had happened to them.
- **C = Clearly communicate the gospel.** As people poured in to investigate the commotion, Peter seized the moment and communicated the message of Jesus clearly, in the power of the Holy Spirit. As a result, 3,000 people began relationships with Jesus!

Why did the 3,000 respond right then? Was it because Peter was such an awesome communicator? No. Was it the 10-day prayer meeting? That had

{ EVERY BELIEVER SHARING
EVERY PERSON HEARING }

something to do with it. The disciples obeyed God's plan. They prayed and waited for the Holy Spirit's power, then went into the city sharing what they knew about Jesus. On every street corner, they saturated Jerusalem so that when Peter communicated the message, tens of thousands of people had already heard individual stories. The result? Harvest!

David Wheeler, director of the Center for Church Planting at Liberty Baptist Theological Seminary in Lynchburg, Va., is regularly asked why a church should do harvest events. His response sheds light on the genius of the Acts 1 and 2 process for reaching people:

> *I tell them it's because events fit all three areas of strategic evangelism: plowing through prayer, planting through personal evangelism, and harvesting through the event. Effective events lead to people beginning a relationship with Christ, which is the first part of making disciples. It's what we're called to do!*[55]

Churches that reach and baptize a large number of lost people use this same strategy. They touch heaven in prayer, mobilize their people to build sharing relationships with lost family, friends, and co-workers, and then they dot their calendars with harvest events. While methods vary, the goal is always to attract the lost and present the plan of salvation through Christ. An evangelism event is simply a tool that allows believers to build relationships with unbelievers. Those relationships lead people to receive Jesus Christ, and new believers lead to church growth when proper follow up is used.

Countless large churches across America grew out of evangelistic events. Larry Wynn, pastor of Hebron Baptist Church in Dacula, Georgia, has used harvest events to build his church from about 100 in Sunday

School, to more than 4,300 in approximately 30 years. Over this timeframe, the church has baptized more than 9,000 people. Wynn said:

> *Creative, cutting edge harvest events have been a key to the growth of Hebron Church and the impact the church has had on the community. Hardly a week goes by that someone doesn't stop me and tell me they came to Christ and were baptized because of a church-sponsored event.*[56]

Thom Rainer, a researcher of effective churches and president of LifeWay Christian Resources, concurred:

> *Harvest events are making a dynamic difference in having an impact on the community with the gospel of Christ. These events are not one-time shots with little or no lasting impact. Indeed, communities are changed for the better before the events begin and long after they are over.*[57]

Pastor Doug Sager is a living example of just how creative these outreach events can become. Sager has used drama to share the good news as he has walked on water, flown via jet pack from balcony to stage and back, raised Lazarus from the dead, and fed 5,000 people. He has played Moses as an adult and as a baby (complete with diaper). Sager has rappelled from the sanctuary ceiling at First Baptist Concord in Tennessee, more times than he can count, even into his late 60s, and all in the name of Jesus. These extravagant performances are part of a big-event ministry, a centerpiece of the church he has pastored for 15 years. Sager has watched his congregation quadruple in size and utilizes harvesting events as effective outreach tools. He noted:

{ EVERY BELIEVER SHARING }
{ EVERY PERSON HEARING }

> *The basic premise is simple — the reason 3,000 people came to Christ on the day of Pentecost is that there were at least 3,000 people there! One of the principles I've used for years is that wherever and however you can get a gathering of people and share the gospel, do it — because there will be people who make a positive response.*[58]

Perhaps you're starting to see past the surface of hosting intentionally evangelistic events. Jim Coldiron, consultant for crusade and revival evangelism for the North American Mission Board and the Billy Graham Evangelistic Association, said that seeing what is beneath a big event is vital:

> *Event evangelism is like an iceberg. The event you see is just about 10 percent of the equation. A successful evangelistic event is about 45 percent preparation, 10 percent proclamation, and 45 percent preservation. In the local churches, the ones that don't prepare are the ones saying event evangelism doesn't work. The ones that prepare are saying it works because they are reaping a harvest.*[59]

Follow Up and Assimilate New Believers

Follow up and assimilation actually begin during the event-preparation process. It's part of the 45 percent of the "iceberg" lying beneath the surface and is key to fulfilling the Great Commission. God has not called us to make "decisions," but rather, to make "disciples." Additionally, follow up and assimilation are paramount to the long-term impact of the event. Over the years, we've seen that churches who make follow up a priority will baptize about 70 percent of those who receive Christ within the six months following their event.

Remember, the work is not over when the event is over. Assimilation is the process of discipleship, helping new believers plug into Bible classes and ministry areas where they can grow in their faith and use their gifts. If new believers are not quickly discipled, their enthusiasm will wane, and their ability to reach others will be delayed. We want to avoid that at all costs! Have decision counselors, individuals trained to assist people in making new professions of faith, ready to follow up for at least four weeks beyond the event.

Initial follow up must be prompt, especially to those who responded to the invitation to become followers of Christ or who sought any form of counsel. The first 48 hours are critical. Can you imagine bringing a baby home from the hospital and not caring for the baby? Of course not! Similarly, these are babes in Christ, and Satan will hate their decision. He will bombard them with doubt and discouragement, so it is vital that someone of strong faith in Christ walk alongside the new believer or transition them to a small group to nurture them.

Preparing Decision Counselors

Even in Christ's day, finding enough trained helpers to bring in the harvest was difficult:

> *The harvest is plentiful, but the laborers are few; therefore beseech the Lord of the harvest to send out laborers into His harvest.*
> **LUKE 10:2**

{ EVERY BELIEVER SHARING }
{ EVERY PERSON HEARING }

Begin recruiting decision counselors 60 days in advance, and train them 30 days prior to a harvest event. Pray about this question: *How many people do I dream will receive Christ at the event?* Whatever the number, train one counselor for every two decisions, and equip your counselors to do four things:

1. Help people pray to receive Christ during the decision time at the event.
2. Assure new believers of their salvation through Scripture, and introduce any follow-up material.
3. Follow up with the new believer within two days and continue contact for at least four weeks using an assimilation program such as *Beginning Steps.*[60]
4. Give each new believer five witnessing booklets, and ask them to identify five friends who need Christ, to pray for them every day, and share the booklets with them.

When identifying and selecting godly decision counselors, ask leaders from past evangelistic events or your church staff to recommend people from your congregation with counseling potential. Enlist the support of Sunday School and small-group Bible study leaders in seeking counselors. Remember to choose counselors of a wide age range, including late teens and college students.

Counseling someone about a personal relationship with Christ may seem daunting, but the great news is that the Holy Spirit—the Ultimate Counselor—handles the encounter. A speaker may share the message and make the truth of Christ clear, but the Holy Spirit is the one who gives the invitation. Teach your decision counselors to allow the Holy Spirit to guide every conversation, being consciously aware of the Spirit's presence. In doing so, the Holy Spirit promises to give the seeker the right questions and provides the well-prepared counselor with the right answers! This includes not just one-on-one counseling, but counseling activities during an evangelistic event.

After counseling takes place, follow up is not an option. It launches the harvest! Never forget that the work of follow up should be bathed in prayer. Seeking the Holy Spirit in each step will determine whether there is long-term success or failure of your efforts. All of your planning and hard work will be sustained if you take the job of follow up seriously.

If you are unsure what resources or steps are needed to adequately prepare for harvesting, a comprehensive list of follow up materials is available in the Recommended Resources section of this book and on the North American Mission Board's website, www.namb.net.[61]

Celebrate Believers' Baptisms

And Jesus came up and spoke to them, saying,
"All authority has been given to Me in heaven and on earth.
Go therefore and make disciples of all the nations, baptizing them in
the name of the Father and the Son and the Holy Spirit,
teaching them to observe all that I commanded you;
and lo, I am with you always, even to the end of the age."
MATTHEW 28:18-20

What would happen if churches across North America held cutting-edge harvest events that had been prayed over, cultivated by engaging with non-believers, and sown with the gospel? Imagine healthy New Testament churches consistently baptizing more people and new churches sprouting up across the continent! An outreach-oriented baptism service is a wonderful way to celebrate decisions for Christ *and* share the gospel with non-Christians at the same time.

Perhaps you've always considered baptism the final step in the evangelism process. Have you ever considered it the first as well? New Christians generally have many friends who do not yet have a personal relationship with Jesus. A baptism service provides this new believer with

{ EVERY BELIEVER SHARING
EVERY PERSON HEARING }

an opportunity to invite friends, family, co-workers and neighbors to hear the gospel. A formal invitation to a baptism service is compelling. If invited, some people who would never go to church otherwise will attend their peer's baptism.

As in any worship service, a celebration of baptism should focus upon drawing people to the Lord Jesus Christ. Every element of the service should funnel people toward allegiance and relationship with God. *The Baptism Celebration* website outlines worship services in three different formats (contemporary, traditional, and blended) designed to bring attendees into a saving relationship with the Lord.[62] Borrow elements from these service plans or revise them as necessary to mesh with your church resources. Most of all, pray first that God will lead and bless as you lift Him up in worship.

As you plan a believers' baptism service, include opportunities for evangelistic outreach. Have each baptismal candidate create a list of individuals they wish to invite, including people who may not know Christ. Use the W.O.R.L.D. acrostic to help build a comprehensive invitation list:

- **W—Workplace.** The workplace provides many opportunities to build relationships with unreached people.
- **O—Organizations.** A garden club, professional organization, the PTA, even the high school band or football team can provide names for your baptism celebration invitation list.
- **R—Relatives.** Many find it difficult to share Christ with relatives. However, we have more evangelistic influence upon family members than any other group of people.
- **L—Lonely People.** This includes newcomers to the community. People are more receptive to spiritual invitations within the first few days or weeks of moving to a new location.
- **D—Daily Contacts.** The checkout person at the grocery store, the bank teller, the mail carrier, etc. can all be invited to a baptism celebration service!

Sample invitations, letters, and other organizational helps are available at www.baptismcelebration.org.

The gospel message can be integrated into the baptism service through varied creative presentations, but there is no greater, indisputable proof of the transforming power of Christ than through testimonies from the new believer. The personal testimony of how the new Christian came to understand and commit to Jesus can be read by the pastor, printed in the service program, or shared by the baptism candidate. You can help new believers plan a clear presentation of how they found new life in Jesus Christ using *The NET* evangelism process mentioned in chapter 3.[63]

Baptism itself is a dramatic presentation of the gospel. It is a picture of salvation as the new believer symbolically professes faith in Jesus Christ. The gospel is the *"power of God for salvation to everyone who believes."*[64] God has placed intrinsic power in the gospel to draw people to Himself. The pastor can explain that the candidate has come to publicly profess faith in Jesus Christ by being baptized. In baptism we state our identification with His death on the cross, burial, and resurrection. In Christ, our old life is buried with Him in death and raised to newness of life through His resurrection, and this new life is available to all who come by faith to Jesus Christ.

Some people who attend the baptism celebration service may show interest in your church. Some might follow the example of those being baptized and commit their lives to Jesus right then and there! Be sure to provide a way for them to make their decisions public, and encourage them to attend a biblically-sound church like yours. Registration of each guest is another vital element of follow up and will enable you to be ready for future contacts.

{ EVERY BELIEVER SHARING }
{ EVERY PERSON HEARING }

Start Something New

Part of God's Plan for Sharing includes the creation of new, innovative harvesting ministries, to me, this is one of the most exhilarating aspects of ministry. When Christ Jesus came into the world, He did a new thing. He created a new covenant with God.[65] When someone accepts Christ as Savior, that individual becomes a new creation in Him. In Acts, Christianity expanded as the gospel crossed old arenas and into new venues. These venues are geographical, numerical and cultural. New visions for a future, new convictions about how to reach more people for Jesus, new understandings about who could be reached in your area, and a new, or perhaps renewed, commitment to evangelize and encourage each of us to explore the creative part of ministry. God has equipped us with particular gifts and expects us to use them.

Churches closely aligned with God's Plan for Sharing will inevitably start many new and culturally-relevant harvesting ministries in response to their unique call, the specific community and opportunity God has placed before them. Imagine as a pastor leading your people to discover your church's particular place in the mission of God. Imagine preaching and leading your church to become more missions-minded while challenging the entire congregation to begin new ministries, teaching units and churches! Launching new small groups and witnessing the revitalization of existing churches are certainly part of evangelistic harvesting.

What do innovative ministries look like for your church? The following suggestions are just a few ways to implement God's Plan for Sharing as you lead your church toward growth through new harvesting efforts.

Ways to Start Something New

- Begin a new innovative worship service on a day or night other than Sunday.

- Start a new Bible study hour for those who cannot make other scheduled times.
- Create a new worship service if you are running out of space in your current worship area.
- Combine prayer and fitness by creating prayerwalking or prayer-cycling groups.
- Begin a new outreach Bible study group in a target area where a church is needed.
- Sponsor a church plant within your region or association.
- Develop and initiate a strategic plan for starting home Bible studies throughout a specific area.
- Enlist your youth and singles to get involved in outreach ministries that take the gospel into unchurched venues.
- Begin Bible study groups or church services for unreached people groups in your ministry area.
- Create a new ministry for multi-housing communities.
- Communicate the gospel through afterschool programs that meet needs in the community.

How is the Lord leading you and your church to try something new? If the prospect of change seems unsettling, rest assured the Lord will not call you into new ministry areas without providing assistance. If you feel He is burdening you and your church to reach the lost in a new way, the laborers and resources will be made available.

Your own church is an excellent place to start. Many new ministries are birthed from within a body of believers. Provide a system for your members to suggest ministries and then serve as leaders. Work with your church's mission education groups and Bible study teachers to discover and plan Bible studies. They will have a valuable perspective on what classes are needed by the membership-at-large.

Local associations are valuable resources as well. They were created for this purpose, and an absolute treasury of resources awaits you through these resource specialists. Churches grouped geographically with yours can support each other through cooperative efforts. Your state convention can also assist with information, training and encouragement. These state leaders are resourced and equipped to help you with God's Plan for Sharing and maximize your creative harvesting efforts.

In addition to these partners, the North American Mission Board provides regional training, materials and information to support evangelism projects and missions throughout the United States and Canada.[66] We have worked hard to provide comprehensive evangelism information for pastors, leaders, church members and missionaries. These tools will help you formulate and implement a vision for reaching the lost in your area.

Harvesting is the tangible result of all our prayer, engaging, and sowing, and it requires commitment motivated by a love for a lost and needy world. We know that in North America, three out of four people will die without a personal relationship with Jesus Christ. And we know that most of them are seeking truth that can only be found in Christ. So, why are we waiting to bring them the gospel?

Every believer is needed in the field. *Your* prayer might lead to the salvation of an entire people group. *Your* relationship with a neighbor might lead that person to ask about what it means to know Jesus as Lord. *You* may mention the gospel to someone who accepts Christ at another church's service. *Your* creative ideas may launch a whole new harvest area.

How are you fulfilling the Great Commission? How is your church doing? Will you consider your role in bringing the hope of Christ to all people of North America?

CHAPTER SIX:
Accepting the Challenge

B efore you put away this book and place it among the other literature on your bookshelf, take a few moments and honestly evaluate your position in God's Plan for Sharing. Think about your personal commitment to the evangelistic process of praying, engaging, sowing, and harvesting. Where is your church in the process, and how can you help your church do better at reaching the lost?

As you think through these questions, listen for the voice of the Holy Spirit. You will hear either affirmation or conviction. Then act upon what He reveals to you.

PRAYING: Every church praying for every lost person.

- In what ways is your church actively praying for lost people?
- How would you describe the demographics of the geographical area surrounding your church?
- How can your church identify the people living near your church to whom you have never reached out?

ENGAGING: Every believer sharing as a trained witness.

- How many believers in your church are trained to share their faith?
- What opportunities or classes can your church offer to help Christians learn about witnessing?
- How can you encourage church members to seek relationships with non-believers in order to bring them to Christ, rather than staying in a "holy huddle" of other Christians?

{ EVERY BELIEVER SHARING
EVERY PERSON HEARING }

SOWING: Every lost person receiving a complete witness.

- When was the last time you specifically shared the gospel with a non-believer?
- Would anyone who is lost—regardless of race, socioeconomic status, or education—feel comfortable in your church? If not, how can you increase that comfort level?
- How can you motivate church members to go out into the field, rather than expecting the lost to come to you?
- How is your church creating intentional opportunities to share the gospel with lost people in your community, county, state and North America?

HARVESTING: Every church harvesting and celebrating every salvation experience.

- Are you seeing people come to Christ through the ministries of your church?
- Are you celebrating those decisions through baptism services to which the lost may come and hear the gospel? How do your church's baptism services celebrate salvation decisions and also offer the gospel message?
- Do you have trained decision counselors who can assist new believers and seekers with questions and discipleship? How can you train more decision counselors to assist new believers and seekers with questions and discipleship?
- Do you or your church leadership embrace the idea of adjusting ministry methods to reach more people, or are you comfortable just doing things the way they've always been done? How do you or your church leaders model openness to adjusting ministry methods to reach more people, rather than being comfortable with doing things the way they've always been done?

What did you hear? Affirmation or conviction?

If we are obedient to God's Word, churches across North America will mobilize to share the redemption of Christ to a desperate world. As you investigate the websites, books, and other resources available, envision how you can help your membership grow in cross cultural-sensitivity, become global citizens with a Christian worldview, and witness effectively about God's unending love. At each step along the way, celebrate your victories while giving God the glory for all He is doing, and will do, in your area.

I cannot imagine a greater blessing than experiencing a first-century surge of Christianity here in our twenty-first century world!

{ EVERY BELIEVER SHARING }
{ EVERY PERSON HEARING }

Guide to References

[1] "Americans Open to Outreach From Churches." LifeWay Research: Nashville, Tennessee, 2009. (http://www.earthtimes.org/articles/show/lifeway-research-survey-americans-open-to-outreach-from-churches,763372.shtml).

[2] Sustainable World, (http://www.sustainableworld.com/data/population/prop_proj_samp.htm).

[3] "Projections of the Population and Components of Change for the United States: 2010 to 2050." Table. US Census Bureau, 2008. (http://www.census.gov/population/www/projections/files/nation/summary/np2008-t1.xls).

[4] Center for Missional Research, North American Mission Board. (www.namb.net/cmr)

[5] Center for Missional Research, North American Mission Board. (www.namb.net/cmr).

[6] Acts 17:6.

[7] 2 Corinthians 4:6.

[8] Center for Missional Research, North American Mission Board.

[9] Murray Moerman, *Discipling Our Nation* (British Columbia, Canada: Church Leadership Library, 2005), pp. 25-26.

[10] Kirin Kalia, ed., Migration Information Source, (http://www.migrationinformation.org/USfocus/display.cfm?id=714#7, 2008).

[11] William Frey, "The Census Projects Minority Surge" (Brookings, August 18, 2008). (http://www.brookings.edu/opinions/2008/0818_census_frey.aspx).

[12] Ibid. p. 11.

[13] Ibid.

[14] Statistics Canada, (http://www.statcan.gc.ca/).

[15] American Religious Data Archive, (www.thearda.com).

[16] Bruce Katz, "The Suburban Challenge." (Brookings, January 26, 2009). (http://www.brookings.edu/opinions/2009/0126_suburbs_katz.aspx).

[17] Ibid.

[18] Matthew 9:36.

[19] Acts 17:16.

[20] Matthew 10, Luke 10.

{ EVERY BELIEVER SHARING }
{ EVERY PERSON HEARING }

[21] Acts 1:8; 2:1.

[22] Acts 2.

[23] Acts 16:6-10.

[24] Luke 10:2b.

[25] John 4:35.

[26] Felicity Dale, *An Army of Ordinary People: Real Stories of Ordinary People Advancing God's Kingdom* (Austin, Texas: Karis Publishing, 2005), p. 85.

[27] Nate Adams, *The Acts 1:8 Challenge: Empowering the Church to be on Mission* (Nashville, Tennessee: LifeWay Press, 2004), p. 150.

[28] Jesse Fletcher, *The Southern Baptist Convention: A Sesquicentennial History* (Nashville, Tennessee: Broadman & Holman Publishers, 1994), p. 34.

[29] Philippians 2:13.

[30] Matthew 15:21-28; Mark 7:24-30.

[31] Oswald Chambers, *My Utmost for His Highest: an Updated Edition in Today's Language* (Nashville, Tennessee: Thomas Nelson Publishers for the Oswald Chambers Publications, 1935, 1992 edition), August 28 devotional.

[32] Norman Grubbs, *Rees Howell Intercessor* (Christian Literature, 1964).

[33] E. G. Carre, *Praying Hyde, Apostle of Prayer* (Bridge Logos Publishers, North Brunswick, NJ 1982, reprint 1999).

[34] Evelyn Christensen, *A Study Guide for Evangelism Praying* (Eugene, Oregon: Harvest House Publishers, 1996), p. 43.

[35] John Piper, *Let the Nations be Glad: The Supremacy of God in Missions* (Grand Rapids, Michigan: Baker Books, 1993. Eleventh printing, 2000), p. 35.

[36] Ephesians 6:18.

[37] Neal Hughes, "The Value of Intentional Prayer Walking in Communities." Unpublished paper. (Atlanta: North American Mission Board, SBC, August 20, 2008), p. 1.

[38] John 5:19.

[39] Minette Drumwright, "Prayer as Missions Strategy." Unpublished paper. (Richmond, Virginia: International Mission Board, SBC, November 1993), pp. 2-3.

[40] Chuck Lawless, *Discipled Warriors: Growing Healthy Churches That Are Equipped for Spiritual Warfare* (Grand Rapids, Michigan: Kregel Publications, 2002), pp. 151-152.

[41] Revelation 4:8.

[42] "O For a Thousand Tongues to Sing." Words: Charles Wesley, 1739. Music: Azmon, Carl G. Gläser, 1828; arranged by Lowell Mason, Modern Psalmist, 1839.

[43] Romans 10:17.

[44] Darrell W. Robinson, *People Sharing Jesus: A Natural, Sensitive Approach to Helping Others Know Christ* (Nashville: Thomas Nelson, 1995) p. 24.

[45] John 4: 1-26.

[46] Romans 1:16, John 16:8-10.

[47] *One-Hour & One-Day Witnessing Workshops*—Workbook, materials. North American Mission Board. (http://www.namb.net/site/c.9qKILUOzEpH/b.224372/k.62A8/OneDayOneHour__Witnessing_Workshop.htm).

[48] *The NET*—Evangelism program. North American Mission Board. (http://www.namb.net/thenet).

[49] Matthew 28:19-20.

[50] John 16:8.

[51] *GPS: God's Plan for Sharing*. Brochure. (Alpharetta, Georgia: North American Mission Board, 2008).

[52] Center for Missional Research, North American Mission Board. (http://www.namb.net/site/c.9qKILUOzEpH/b.1648807/k.8318/Center_for_Missional_Research__Statistics_and_Studies_on_Church_Culture_Community.htm).

[53] Acts 9.

[54] Acts 2.

[55] David Wheeler—Interviewed by Jerry Pipes. May 2005.

[56] Larry Wynn—Interviewed by Victor Lee. October 2007.

[57] Jerry Pipes, "The Case for Event Evangelism." Article. (Lawrenceville, Georgia: Jerry Pipes Productions, August 2005).

[58] Doug Sader—Interviewed by Victor Lee. October 2007.

[59] Jim Coldiron—Interviewed by Victor Lee. October 2007.

[60] *Beginning Steps*—Workbook. North American Mission Board.

[61] North American Mission Board. (www.namb.net).

[62] Baptism Celebration. (www.baptismcelebration.org).

[63] *The NET.* North American Mission Board.

[64] Romans 1:16.

[65] Luke 23:45.

[66] North American Mission Board. (www.namb.net).

{ EVERY BELIEVER SHARING }
{ EVERY PERSON HEARING }

Additional Recommended Resources

Chapter 2: Praying

Disciple's Prayer Life, LifeWay

Prayer 101: What Every Intercessor Needs to Know, Elaine Helms, (www.wmustore.com)

Praying Your Friends to Christ, (www.ncbaptist.org)

Prayerwalking Made Simple, (www.gabaptist.org)

Follow Me, Randy Sprinkle, (www.wmustore.com)

Taking Prayer to the Streets — Bible Study, NAMB

Taking Prayer to the Streets — Pocket Guide, NAMB

Who's in Your Wallet?, NAMB

316 Prayer Cards, NAMB

Returning to Holiness, Gregory Frizzell, The Master Design, Fulton, KY

Study Guide for Evangelism Praying, Evelyn Christenson (unitedprayerministry.org)

Experiencing God, Henry Blackaby, LifeWay

Chapter 3: Engaging

CROSS Evangelism Training, NAMB

Got Life, (gotlifeministries.com)

One-Hour Witnessing Workshop, NAMB (namb.net/onedaywitness)

One-Day Witnessing Workshop, NAMB, (namb.net/onedaywitness)

The NET, NAMB

HeartCall, NAMB

RELAY, NAMB

God's Special Plan for Children, NAMB

Connect, (connectwithgod.com)

FAITH, LifeWay

{ EVERY BELIEVER SHARING
EVERY PERSON HEARING }

Share Jesus Without Fear, LifeWay

G.R.O.W., LifeWay

Soul-Winning Commitment Day, (thebigday.org)

Research and Demographics/Center for Missional Research, (namb.net/cmr)

Apologetics, (4truth.net)

Chapter 4: Sowing

Eternal Life, NAMB

One-Day Witnessing Card, NAMB, (namb.net/onedaywitness)

An Important Question for an Important Person, NAMB

Your Life: A New Beginning, NAMB

Servanthood Evangelism Manual, NAMB

High Impact Events Manual, NAMB

Good News for You Bible Study, Charles Brock, (churchgrowthinternational.com)

Chapter 5: Harvesting

Revival Preparation Manual, NAMB

Crusade Manual, NAMB

FiSH – Studentz.com, (www.studentz.com)

High Impact Events Manual, NAMB

Evangelism Planner, NAMB

Evangelism Response Center, (www.erconline.net)

Seven Steps for Planting Churches, NAMB (ChurchPlantingVillage.net)

Basic Training for Church Planters (Contact your state church planting leader)

Personal Commitment Guide—A counseling booklet. NAMB

Beginning Steps for New Believers—A study guide for new Believers, NAMB

World's Greatest Adventure—Beginning steps for children, NAMB

Celebrate Baptism, (baptismcelebration.org)
The Church Planting Journey: An Introduction for Sponsors and Partners,
(churchplantingvillage.net)

To order priced products from the North American Mission Board, call
toll-free, 1 866 407-NAMB (6262), or visit *nambstore.com.*

To obtain free church planting resources from the North American
Mission Board, visit *churchplantingvillage.net.*

To order priced products from LifeWay Christian Resources, call toll-free,
1 800 448-8032, or visit *lifewaychristianstores.com.*

{ EVERY BELIEVER SHARING }
{ EVERY PERSON HEARING }